SCULPTURE
BEHIND THE SCENES
ANDREW PEKARIK

D1364270

HYPERION BOOKS FOR CHILDREN

NEW YORK

SPECIAL THANKS:

I want to thank the team at Hyperion, who helped me at every stage, especially Liz Gordon and Andrea Cascardi for their expert editorial advice; Lauri Greaton and Doug Freedman for their patient dedication to so many details; and Ellen Friedman for her imaginative design.

First Edition

1 3 5 7 9 10 8 6 4 2

Library of Congress Cataloging-in-Publication Data

Pekarik, Andrew.
 Behind the scenes: sculpture /Andrew Pekarik.
 p. cm.
 Summary: Discusses sculpture from a sculptor's viewpoint and uses specific examples to point out how to discover the details in a sculpture.
 ISBN 1-56282-294-2 (trade) — ISBN 1-56282-295-0 (lib. bdg.)
 1. Sculpture — Juvenile literature. [1. Sculpture.
2. Art appreciation.] I. Title. II. Title: Sculpture.
NB1143.P45 1992
730'.1'1 — dc20 92-52988 CIP AC

Behind the Scenes is a production of Learning Designs, Inc., and WNET/THIRTEEN. Funders for the series include McDonald's Family Restaurants, the National Endowment for the Arts, the Corporation for Public Broadcasting, the Arthur Vining Davis Foundations, the John D. and Catherine T. MacArthur Foundation, the Andrew W. Mellon Foundation, the Bingham Trust, the Nathan Cummings Foundation, the Andy Warhol Foundation for the Visual Arts, and the George Gund Foundation.

ACKNOWLEDGMENTS

Cover: *Unending Revolution of Venus, Plants, and Pendulum* by Nancy Graves, 1992. Clockworks by Saff Tech CLOCKWORKS. © 1992 Saff Tech Arts/Nancy Graves. Photograph by Sam Kwong.

Page 4: *Unidentified Object* by Isamu Noguchi, 1979. The Metropolitan Museum of Art. Gift of the Isamu Noguchi Foundation, Inc., 1981. (1981.131) Photograph © 1986 Metropolitan Museum of Art.

Page 6: *Little Fourteen-Year-Old Dancer* by Edgar Degas, 1878–81. Collection of Mr. and Mrs. Paul Mellon, Upperville, Virginia.

Page 7: *Little Fourteen-Year-Old Dancer* by Edgar Degas, ca. 1880–81. The Metropolitan Museum of Art, Bequest of Mrs. H. O. Havemeyer, 1929. The H. O. Havemeyer Collection. Photograph © 1981 Metropolitan Museum of Art.

Page 8: Maquette for *Guitar* by Pablo Picasso, early 1912. Collection, The Museum of Modern Art, New York. Gift of the artist. Photograph © 1992, The Museum of Modern Art, New York.

Page 10: *Bicycle Wheel* by Marcel Duchamp, 1951, third version. Collection, The Museum of Modern Art, New York. The Sidney and Harriet Janis Collection. Photograph © 1992, The Museum of Modern Art, New York.

Page 11: *Bonseki Named Suenomatsu-Yama.* Artist unknown, ca. 16th century. Courtesy of the Hongwanji Archives, Kyoto, Japan.

Page 15: Chartres Cathedral, West (or Royal) Portal. Artist unknown, ca. 12th century. Giraudon/Art Resource, New York.

Page 16: *Large Torso: Arch* by Henry Moore, 1962–63. Collection, The Museum of Modern Art, New York. Mrs. Simon Guggenheim Fund. Photograph © 1992, The Museum of Modern Art, New York.

Page 17: *Monument to Balzac* by Auguste Rodin, 1897–98. Collection, The Museum of Modern Art, New York. Presented in memory of Curt Valentin by his friends. Photograph © 1992, The Museum of Modern Art, New York.

Page 18: *Bird in Space* by Constantin Brancusi, ca. 1924. Philadelphia Museum of Art: The Louise and Walter Arensberg Collection.

Page 19: *Bird in Space* by Constantin Brancusi, 1925. Courtesy of National Gallery of Art, Washington, D.C. Gift of Eugene and Agnes E. Meyer.

Page 20: *Dancing Ten-armed Ganesha with Earthly and Celestial Musicians.* Artist unknown, 8th century. Courtesy of The Asia Society, New York. Mr. and Mrs. John D. Rockefeller 3rd Collection. (1979.13) Photograph by Otto E. Nelson.

Page 22: *Hanging Spider* by Alexander Calder, ca. 1940. Collection of Whitney Museum of American Art, New York. Mrs. John B. Putnam Bequest. Photograph © 1992 Geoffrey Clements, New York.

Page 24: *Unending Revolution of Venus, Plants, and Pendulum* by Nancy Graves, 1992. Clockworks by Saff Tech CLOCKWORKS. © 1992 Saff Tech Arts/Nancy Graves. Photograph by Sam Kwong.

Page 28: *Statue of Liberty,* Liberty Island, New York, Frédéric-Auguste Bartholdi, dedicated 1886. Photograph courtesy of HABS/HAER Collections, Washington, D.C. Photograph by Jack Boucher, 1978.

Page 30: *Floor-Burger (Giant Hamburger)* by Claes Oldenburg, 1962. Reproduced with permission of the artist. Photograph courtesy of Art Gallery of Ontario, Toronto, Ontario, Canada.

Page 32: *The Saint Padmasambhava.* Artist unknown, 17th century. Los Angeles County Museum of Art, gift of Corky and Don Whitaker. Photograph © 1989.

Page 34: *Soap Bubble Set* by Joseph Cornell, 1936. Wadsworth Atheneum, Hartford, Connecticut. Gift of Henry and Walter Keney. Photograph © Wadsworth Atheneum.

Page 36: *The Roden Crater Project* in Arizona by James Turrell. Ongoing project. Reproduced with permission of the artist. Photographs © 1987 Dick Wiser.

Page 40: *Reclining Camel.* Artist unknown. The Seattle Art Museum, Gift of Mrs. John C. Atwood, Jr. (69.8). Photograph by Paul Macapia.

Page 42: *Oath-Taking Figure.* Artist unknown, 19th century. Collection, Musee de L'Homme, Paris, France.

Page 44: *Pietà* by Michelangelo, 1498–99. Scala/Art Resource, New York.

Page 46: *Man Pointing* by Alberto Giacometti, 1947. Collection, The Museum of Modern Art, New York. Gift of Mrs. John D. Rockefeller 3rd. Photograph © 1992, The Museum of Modern Art, New York.

Page 48: The Iris and B. Gerald Cantor Roof Garden. View to the South, with *Becca* by David Smith, 1965. The Metropolitan Museum of Art (1972.127). Photograph © 1989 Metropolitan Museum of Art.

Page 52: *Mask of Born-to-Be-Head-of-the-World* (two views). Artist unknown. Neg. #4577(2) and Neg. #4578(2), Courtesy Department of Library Services, American Museum of Natural History. Photographs by Lynton Gardiner, © American Museum of Natural History.

Page 54: *Poseidon of Artemisium.* Artist unknown. Courtesy of the National Archaelogical Museum, Athens, Greece.

Page 57: *Tilted Arc* by Richard Serra, installed in Federal Plaza, New York, New York 1981–89. Photograph courtesy of The Pace Gallery.

Page 59: *What It's Like, What It Is, 3* by Adrian Piper, 1991. Courtesy John Weber Gallery, New York.

TABLE OF CONTENTS

INTRODUCTION

When many people hear the word *art* they think of painting because the terms *artist* and *painter* are often thought of as the same thing. But sculpture is also a very important art.

Paintings and sculptures are different in many ways. Some of the differences are obvious. A painting is usually flat and attached to or part of a wall, whereas a sculpture is usually a freestanding object or one that stands out from a wall. When you look at a painting you usually stand in one place, but when you look at a sculpture you usually have to move around it to see it all. Sculptures are more physical than paintings because they stand by themselves, are often made of heavy materials, and invite you to touch and handle them.

Sculptures have presence. They are hard to photograph and sometimes hard to remember accurately. You have to be standing next to them, sharing the same space, in order to fully understand what they are about and what they have to say. So in reading this book you will have to use your imagination. Only when you stand in the same space with a sculpture will you be able to fully explore and discover this art form.

This book, we hope, will introduce you to principles that can guide the way you experience sculpture. You can carry the investigation further by looking at the sculptures in person and by reading more about the artists and about the history of art. Many of the artists mentioned in this book are living Americans. If you do not have the chance to visit the museums that own the works photographed here, go to your local art museum and look at other sculptures by the artists who interest you or see if you can use your new knowledge of how to look at sculpture with works by other artists. As soon as you start thinking about sculpture you will notice it all around you— at home, in school, in the park, and in public buildings. You may also want to create sculptures of your own. We hope that this book will make sculpture more interesting and fun for you.

TRANSFORMATION OF MATERIALS

Making sculpture is all about changing one thing into something else. That transformation can be complete and dramatic, such as taking a lump of clay and shaping it into a figure. Or the change can be small and subtle; even taking a rock, putting it on a pedestal, and giving it a title can make people think about it in a new way.

This act of transformation always requires creativity and imagination, and sometimes it also demands great technical skill derived from long practice and training. Part of the delight that you can discover in a work of sculpture comes from an appreciation of how it was made.

REMOVING

One of the most basic sculptural methods is to take a piece of natural material, most commonly stone or wood, and to selectively remove parts of it until a new form, the sculpture, is revealed.

Some sculptors plan their work by making drawings, either on paper or on the thing to be carved. The most famous European sculptor, Michelangelo, made simple sketches and was able to envision the finished object inside the block of stone. Other sculptors do not start out with a definite shape in mind but let the idea of the object develop gradually as they work. A sculptor who followed this method was Isamu Noguchi.

Noguchi felt deep passion for the physical material of the stone he carved. Noguchi said, "I attack the stone with violence. Is this to tame it or to awaken myself? To fulfill the potential in the stone I seek a power to cope by any means. Destruction is then the road to creation." As he alternately worked on and thought about a sculpture, he would discover how to respond to the challenges of the boulder in a unique way.

Unidentified Object, Isamu Noguchi, 1979
Black basalt, height (with base): 222"

The basic shape of Noguchi's sculpture was formed by nature. The brown surface of the boulder is the outer layer of the rock. Noguchi met its challenge by selectively removing sections of the stone to reveal the black rock inside. Perched on a tall pedestal, this sculpture seems to hold some important secret message, but the artist was not willing to identify it and so he called it *Unidentified Object.*

You have to use your imagination to deal with this mystery object. What does the shape look like to you? Could it be a huge fossil, like a dinosaur bone? Are rocks the bones of the earth? Noguchi's precise cuts and carvings highlight the beauty of the stone by revealing its surprising black interior. Do these marks look like decay? Like the result of something that ate into the bone? Like damaged areas where another rock knocked against it? Although rocks are old and tough, they are not unchanging and eternal. They can be worn smooth over time or broken. People, especially artists, have always insisted on demonstrating their power to change even nature's most enduring elements.

An artist who works with a soft substance, especially clay or wax, can freely form almost any shape and is not dependent on the size, shape, or structure of a particular piece of wood or stone. A sculptor who models flexible material usually begins with an armature—a framework of wood or metal—to provide support. Objects made of soft material are fragile but can be preserved by metal casting with materials such as bronze. The casting process usually requires that a mold be made around the original material. The mold then gives shape to molten (liquified) metal, which eventually cools off and hardens in the form of the original sculpture.

The impressionist artist Edgar Degas, who is most famous for his paintings and drawings, also made sculptures from wax. The material was so soft that it recorded every detail of the artist's touch, down to his fingerprints. Amazingly, some of these fragile sculptures still survive in reasonably good condition. None of them were made into bronze during Degas's lifetime, probably in part because he was not willing to consider them completely finished.

Little Fourteen-Year-Old Dancer, Edgar Degas, 1878–81
Yellow wax, tulle skirt, and satin hair ribbon, height: 39"

MODELING

On one occasion, Degas announced that after twenty reworkings he was ready to have one of his sculptures cast into bronze so that it could be sold. But the very next day he rolled the wax back up into a ball and started over, saying to his friend Ambroise Vollard, "You think above all of what it was worth, Vollard, but if you had given me a hatful of diamonds my happiness would not have equalled that which I derived from demolishing [the figure] and starting over." Obviously, for Degas the pleasure of forming a sculpture outweighed the value of selling it.

Nevertheless, bronze versions were made after Degas's death, most of them from copies of copies. These bronzes preserved much detail but lost some of the subtle touches of the original, in the same manner that a photograph loses some of the nuances of an original painting.

A sculptor who wants to work in a soft, responsive material such as wax knows that the work will be very difficult to preserve unless it is reproduced in a more solid substance. Although two Degas sculptures are shown here only in photographs, can you detect any differences between the original wax version and the bronze reproduction?

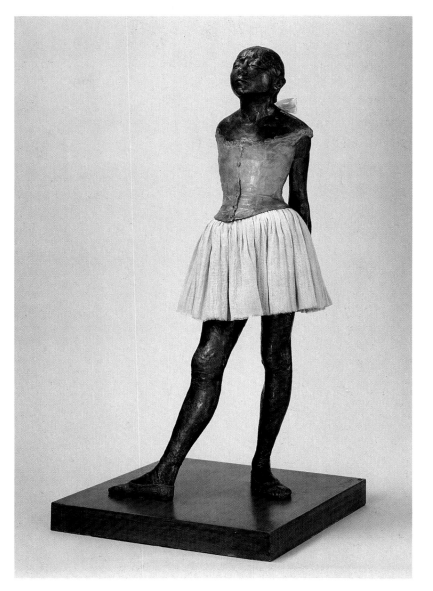

Little Fourteen-Year-Old Dancer, Edgar Degas, 1880–81
Bronze (cast 1922), tulle skirt, and satin hair ribbon, height: 39"

CONSTRUCTION

In the European tradition, sculpture was made either by carving or by modeling, until Pablo Picasso and his friend Georges Braque started constructing sculptures out of cardboard and paper in 1912. Braque's sculptures have not survived, but Picasso preserved his, one of which is now in the Museum of Modern Art in New York City.

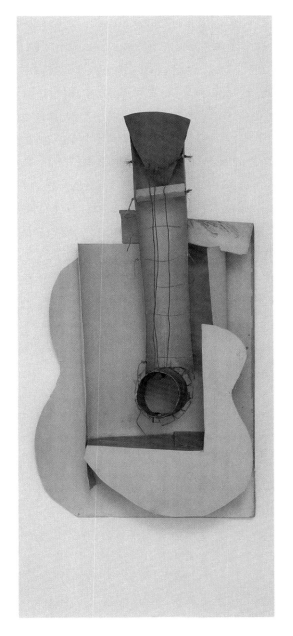

Maquette for Guitar, Pablo Picasso, 1912
Cardboard and string (restored), 26 1/8" x 13 3/8" x 7 5/8"

Picasso's sculpture is pieced together, rather than carved or shaped, and is made using simple methods and very ordinary materials. With this modest guitar Picasso shifted the emphasis of sculpture from bronze casting and stone carving to making assemblages from everyday materials. This broke an artistic pattern that had prevailed in the Western world for thousands of years.

This sculpture is an extension of Picasso's painting style: It is a clever appreciation of the shape of a guitar without being an exact duplicate of an actual guitar. The musical instrument is referred to by its most distinctive shapes, such as the double curve of the body, the sound hole, the vertical neck, the strings, and the raised sides. Some parts of a guitar are not shown, and the pieces that are shown do not correspond in size or position to their counterparts on a real guitar. But you cannot mistake the subject of the sculpture.

By putting together this sculpture from various pieces representing different scales (like parts from guitars of many different sizes), Picasso asks you to consider along with him how a guitar is formed in three-dimensional space and how it is perceived. The sculpture is an attempt to describe "guitarness," or what a guitar means, rather than to portray an actual guitar.

Marcel Duchamp went one step further than Picasso with sculptures he called ready-mades. These were common objects that he selected and displayed as art. The first was *Bicycle Wheel,* chosen in 1913.

Duchamp rejected the idea that an artist must produce masterpieces. He thought that an artist ought to be able to select any object out of the vast number that surround people at all times. If the artist wanted to call it art, who could object? Of course, people did object when he mounted a bicycle wheel on a kitchen stool like an elaborate sculpture on a pedestal. But Duchamp believed their opinions about good taste were just prejudices. What is special about the bicycle wheel on a pedestal? It's not the shape or scale or surface of the object, or the way it was made or what it suggests about perception or movement. *Bicycle Wheel* is art if it forces you to think about art, to consider what art is and what it means to you.

Duchamp realized that what is really important about an art object is not just the object itself but the way people think about it. Art is an experience, not a thing.

Bicycle Wheel, Marcel Duchamp, 1951
(third version, after lost original of 1913)
Assemblage: metal wheel, 25 1/2" diameter, mounted on painted wood stool 23 3/4" high;
overall: 50 1/2" x 25 1/2" x 15 5/8"

SELECTION

In 1913 Europe, choosing an existing object and calling it art was a very new idea, but in Asia it was already a very old idea. Nearly five hundred years earlier, in Japan, an anonymous artist selected a rock, put it on a tray, and gave it a name, making it an art object. Suenomatsu-Yama is the name of a mountain in Miyazaki Prefecture in Japan and means "mountain with pines on top." It appeared frequently in poetry in the phrase "when the ocean waves cover Suenomatsu Mountain," describing something absolutely impossible. Does it look to you like a tall mountain?

The artistic value of this sculpture comes from more than the initial act of selection by the person who put the rock on the tray. Everyone who treasured and preserved this object from generation to generation contributed to its status as art. You, too, can choose an object and call it art, but only time will tell if anyone else agrees.

Bonseki Named Suenomatsu-Yama, artist unknown, sixteenth century
Rock: 6 1/4" x 9 1/2"; tray: 15 3/4" diameter

FORM IN SPACE

Every sculpture is three-dimensional. Sculpture communicates through its shape and the way that shape changes the space around it. The overall form of a sculpture is usually the first thing that you notice about it. Often it takes the form of something obvious and familiar, such as a person or an animal or a geometric shape. But sometimes a sculpture has a completely original shape that does not look like anything else. No matter how familiar or unfamiliar the subject may be, however, you can still appreciate a sculpture by considering the general properties of its form.

A sculpture's general properties include its cut, outer shape, use of interior space, and the relationship of its shape to gravity and movement.

CONTOUR:
THE OUTSIDE SHAPE

Three large sculptures carved in stone stand on the left side of the central door of the west portal of Chartres Cathedral in France, one of the most beautiful buildings in the world. They represent two kings and a queen from the Old Testament of the Bible.

The sculptor, who carved them in the 1140s, made them especially tall and thin. Do you notice anything unusual about their feet? The figures protrude as little as possible from their pedestals, so they appear to be part of the round columns.

Why did the sculptor want the figures to be part of the columns? One reason might be that medieval Christians believed that the kings and queens mentioned in the Old Testament of the Bible pointed the way to the birth of Jesus Christ, the son of God in Christian religions. They were literally the pillars on which Christian theology was built.

Why are the figures so elongated? One important reason is mathematical. The sculptor didn't care as much about the human proportions as he did about an ideal system of proportion. In the process of designing harmonious shapes, whether they were buildings or sculptures, the ancient Greeks discovered that two given dimensions, called L and S, looked best together when the ratio of the longer length, L, to the shorter one, S, was the same as the ratio of the sum of the two lengths, S+L, to L, the longer length. This ideal ratio works out mathematically to be approximately 8 to 5, or 1.6 to 1. This is called the golden section and was used by artists and architects long after its discovery by the ancient Greeks.

Medieval sculptors were deeply interested in mathematics. Every part of the cathedral was carefully calculated according to geometric rules. The artists and architects felt that the act of bringing order to stone—by measuring it, carving it, and positioning it to form pillars, walls, and ultimately cathedrals—was the human expression of God's work as Creator, by which He gave harmony and meaning to the world.

The Old Testament kings and queen at Chartres were shaped to follow the golden section. Notice their prominent bent arms. Use a centimeter ruler to measure the figure in the center from the tip of his halo to the top of his waist (S). Write that number down and then measure from the top of his waist to the tip of his toes (L). Write that number down. Now use a calculator to divide the waist-to-toe measurement (L) into the overall height (S+L). The answer should be approximately 1.6.

Chartres Cathedral, West (or Royal) Portal, 1140s

ENCLOSING:
THE SPACE INSIDE

Large Torso: Arch, Henry Moore, 1962–63
Bronze, 78 1/8" x 59 1/8" x 51 1/4"

Some sculptures encourage you to think about the space enclosed by, or inside, the sculpture as well as about its outer shape.

The sculptor Henry Moore gave one of his sculptures a name that suggests the importance of its inside space as well as its outside shape. He called it *Large Torso: Arch. Large Torso* refers to its outside shape and suggests a body. Does that make sense to you? Does the sculpture remind you of a part of the body, maybe a bone? It does seem to stand solidly, as if on two legs.

But the second part of the name, *Arch,* encourages you to look at it another way and to think of it as an archway that you can enter. That idea is weakened a little by the pedestal it stands on, but if this tall sculpture were standing directly on the ground, it would seem quite natural to walk through it.

Can you remember when you were very small and played a game with adults who were so tall that their spread legs were simultaneously a large torso and an arch? How did that make you feel? Does this sculpture give you the same kind of feeling? Does it make you want to wrap your arms around it and try to climb up it?

Weight is an essential feature of all objects. Gravity pulls everything, including you, down toward the earth. Artists can create the impression of heavy weight or lightness in a sculpture. The statues at Chartres draw your attention toward structure and shape, rather than toward weight. The Old Testament kings and queen, although they are made of stone, look weightless, primarily because they seem to be floating.

Auguste Rodin's statue of the French novelist Honoré de Balzac is a massive, looming presence, nearly nine feet tall. When placed on a base, as it is here, it is even taller. By showing Balzac wrapped in a massive cloak that hides his arms and legs, Rodin presents him as a solid column of bronze. His right foot is forward, past the edge of the base. Try covering his foot with your finger and notice how different the statue seems. Does this change its feeling of being rooted to the ground? Does it change its sense of movement?

The shape of the sculpture is different, depending on the direction from which you view it. But from all sides Balzac seems especially heavy and solid, literally a man of substance.

His head tilts up as if he were looking into the distance. What do you think is on his mind? Rodin felt that Balzac was a visionary of tremendous stature and power who was firmly grounded in the present. Does the shape of the statue reflect that view?

Monument to Balzac, Auguste Rodin,1897–98
Bronze (cast 1954), 106" high, at base 48 1/4" x 41"

WEIGHT

REACHING

By making his statue of Balzac resemble a wide, solid column of bronze, Rodin emphasized its weight. In many sculptures by Constantin Brancusi, a thin, pointed shape creates a feeling of lightness that symbolizes the breaking of the bonds of gravity.

This sleek, polished bronze sculpture gives the impression that it is moving through space rather than occupying it. It seems to extend beyond itself, launched from its base, taking off to grow and soar.

This sculpture was inspired by the Romanian legend of a miraculous golden bird, called Maiastra, whose feathers shine at night and who is a symbol of spirituality. The sculptor was so fascinated with this idea that he made many versions of *Bird in Space,* both in bronze and in marble.

Does it look like a bird? You can identify the beak and the tail, but there are no wings. Most people imagining a sculpture of a bird in flight would focus on the wings. Brancusi realized that the more essential feature was the sense of soaring through space. His sculpture tries to give you that feeling, rather than the image of a flying bird.

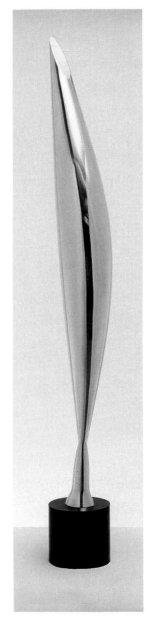

Bird in Space, Constantin Brancusi, ca.1924
Polished bronze, (base) marble and oak, height: 49 3/4"

18

In the bronze versions of *Bird in Space,* the shiny metal surface is covered with reflections. As you move around this sculpture, its surface keeps shifting according to the light and colors of the room. The shiny surface also de-emphasizes the edges of the shape. Which version do you think gives more of a feeling of life and movement?

When this statue was imported into the United States in 1926, the U.S. Customs inspector (who was an amateur sculptor) claimed that it was not art but just metal and hence was subject to import duty. Brancusi objected and the case went to trial. It took two years for the court to decide that, yes, it was art. This was an important moment in the history of art in the United States because it forced people to debate whether or not a sculpture had to look like a familiar object in order to be art.

Bird in Space, Constantin Brancusi, 1925
Marble, (base) stone and wood, height: 136 1/2"

MOVEMENT

Most sculptures are made from solid materials that are enduring but lifeless. Artists who wish to emphasize the unchanging nature of their objects can make them seem rigid and fixed, like the pillarlike statues in the doorway at Chartres. Others try to use solid material to demonstrate energy and movement.

This sculpture was made in India in the eighth century to fit into the wall of a temple. It depicts a deity named Ganesha as a figure with two legs, ten arms, and an elephant's head. Ganesha is the son of the great Hindu god Shiva.

There are stories explaining how Ganesha came to have the head of an elephant. Some say that he made Shiva so angry that Shiva cut off his head. When Ganesha's mother protested, Shiva replaced Ganesha's

Dancing Ten-armed Ganesha with Earthly and Celestial Musicians,
unknown artist, central India, eighth century
Pinkish beige sandstone, height: 49 1/2"

head with the first one that he could find—an elephant head. Ganesha is regarded by Hindus as the remover of obstacles and the patron god of students and teachers.

This version of Ganesha shows him dancing to drum music played by the small musicians who are figured around him on the sculpture. His arms, all ten of them, wave gracefully, his body sways, and his trunk swings joyously in a sweeping curve. Even his elephant ears seem to be flapping in time to the music. Would you agree that this statue has rhythm, like music does? How can sandstone be like music?

This sculpture is a massive block of stone. It is so heavy that you would need a small crane to move it and so durable that it has lasted for more than 1,200 years with only minor damage. (The upper part of the halo is broken off.) But does it look heavy? Can you imagine this sculpture of Ganesha actually dancing?

For centuries, artists made sculptures, such as Dancing Ten-armed Ganesha, that cleverly suggested movement. But in 1930 an American artist working in Paris, Alexander Calder, started making sculptures that actually did move, with the aid of electric motors. However, he did not like the regularity of their motion or the unreliability of the motors, so he next created sculptures that were so delicately balanced that just a touch of a breeze would move them in unpredictable ways. These sculptures were given the name *mobiles*. Calder said, "When everything goes right a mobile is a piece of poetry that dances with the joy of life and surprises."

Calder named one of his mobiles *Hanging Spider*. This sculpture hangs from the ceiling and seems to quiver slightly from the movement of air around it, as if it were expecting something. Can you imagine a spider patiently waiting for some unsuspecting fly to land in its

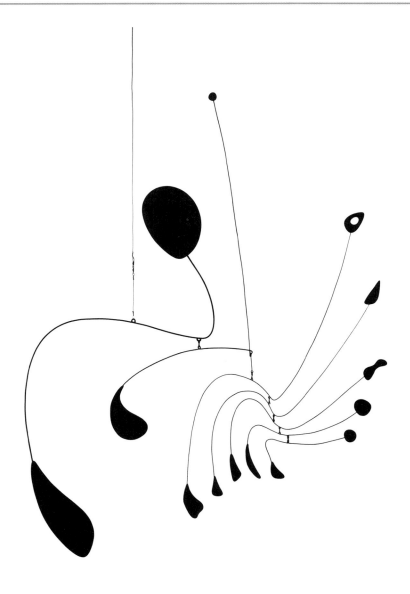

MOVING SCULPTURE

Hanging Spider, Alexander Calder, ca. 1940
Painted sheet metal and wire, 49 1/2" x 35 1/2"

web? When it starts to turn, from a stronger current of air, the five smaller wires on the right twist as a group, bouncing gently up and down and clinking against one another. Could they be the spider's legs? One tall wire sticks straight up like an antenna. Where is the spider's body? Does it have an eye?

If you were the artist who made this mobile, would you have given it a different name? When you were a baby, too small to walk or even crawl, you spent the day lying in a crib. Did anyone hang a mobile over your head for you to look at? How would you have felt if it had been Calder's sculpture?

BALANCE

Contemporary American sculptor Nancy Graves's sculpture is a bold example of balance and counter-balance and the illusion of weightlessness and movement. In part it is a clock powered by two weights that slowly move toward the floor. One weight looks like a horseshoe crab, the other like a bronze head. The hands of the clock, in the center, are hard to find because they are very crooked. This is not so much a useful timepiece as it is a work of art.

The clock is a sculpture about time. The artist has included copies of ancient Egyptian and Roman portraiture as well as examples of European and Islamic architecture.

Unending Revolution of Venus, Plants, and Pendulum, Nancy Graves, 1992/Clockworks by Saff Tech CLOCKWORKS
Bronze, brass, stainless steel, aluminum, and enamel, 96" x 84" x 48"

They are like fragments torn from ruins all over the world.

Linked together in a circle by a massive rope, the pieces look like they are in motion, flying and tumbling as if they were being juggled by an invisible force. You could say that they symbolize the turbulence of time as it witnesses civilizations rise, fall, and give way to others in a never-ending cycle.

Because its parts seem to be flying or moving, the sculpture gives the impression of being light when actually it is very heavy. Most of the objects were cast directly in bronze. Some of the pieces were cast from natural objects, such as palm fronds. Others, such as the Egyptian heads, were cast from original creations or found objects. Graves carefully welded these sections together to construct the complete work. The paint on the bronze sculpture helps tie together the parts by influencing the movement of your eye as you look at and follow each color. This, too, helps bring the parts together into an integrated whole. Graves's main concern was maintaining an equilibrium, or balance, of all the parts so that they would seem to be swirling on their own while creating a unified feeling as a single sculpture.

SCALE

Do you think that the size of a sculpture influences the way that you will respond to it? A huge object forces you to look at it, and the larger it is the more fascinating it will probably be. Is that one reason that dinosaur skeletons are more immediately interesting than squirrel skeletons?

A very small sculpture can also be interesting because its tiny size focuses your attention and draws you close to it. Imagine a sculpture as small as a single grain of rice. You would need a magnifying glass just to see it, but it would be an amazing object.

Sculptures that are approximately human in scale also have a particular effect. They tend to make you feel comfortable standing near them, because their size is familiar.

What happens when a statue of medium size represents something huge or minute? For instance, model ships or dollhouses are not especially small, but they are much smaller than an actual ship or a real house. Similarly, a four-foot-long shoe would certainly make an impression.

LARGE SCALE

Holding a 10-inch-high model of the Statue of Liberty in your hand is a completely different experience from standing at the base of the actual statue and staring up at its massive form. In fact, the Statue of Liberty is so tall that you cannot see it very well when you stand on its tiny island. The statue was meant to be appreciated from a distance, either from the tip of Manhattan Island or from a boat in New York harbor. Why do you think it was made so big?

The French sculptor Frédéric-Auguste Bartholdi, who created the Statue of Liberty, made the first version out of clay. It was only 10 3/8 inches tall. Bartholdi wanted to make a great monument to commemorate a great

Statue of Liberty, Frédéric-Auguste Bartholdi, dedicated 1886
Copper sheets on iron armature, height: 151'

principle—liberty—and although a 10-inch sculpture might be admired, it is too small to make much of a public impression.

Colossal sculptures have been made throughout history. Bartholdi was especially impressed by ancient Egyptian pyramids, temples, and huge statues, such as the Sphinx.

Bartholdi enlarged his sculpture in stages. The second stage was a clay model 49 1/4 inches high, from which he constructed a 9-foot 4-inch version in plaster, then a 36-foot-tall version in plaster, and finally full-scale sections in plaster on massive wooden frames. (The completed full-scale statue is 151 feet high from toe to top of torch, more than 175 times the height of the first model.) Each enlargement required more than nine thousand measurements and constant adjustments.

Thin copper sheets (only a tenth of an inch thick) were bent and hammered over the plaster. This thin skin needed a strong and complicated structure to hold it up inside. Alexandre-Gustave Eiffel, the French engineer who designed the Eiffel Tower in Paris, devised an internal structure made out of wrought iron. The statue itself was constructed in Paris and given as a gift from the French people to America. Most Americans were not enthusiastic about the gift at first and only reluctantly put up the money to build the pedestal for it.

From the beginning the sculptor intended visitors to enjoy the statue from the inside by means of the double stairway of 168 steps that spirals up the interior. The impression of the inside is confusing. It is like being in a metal cave. At the top you can see the harbor from Liberty's crown—a giant's-eye view.

SCALE AND SUBJECT

Giant Hamburger, Claes Oldenburg, 1962
Canvas filled with foam rubber and paper cartons, painted with liquitex and latex, 52" high x 84" diameter

Although the Statue of Liberty is amazingly tall, its great size does not seem odd or unnatural because we are accustomed to heroic, larger-than-life human figures. Much stranger would be a colossal statue of a cow or a dog. The American artist Claes Oldenburg has made many works that are surprising because they transform unlikely, small objects into large-scale sculptures. By changing their scale he changes their meaning.

Oldenburg created a seven-foot-wide hamburger out of painted canvas stuffed with foam. This is a long way from the Statue of Liberty! The sculpture is lumpy and made of ordinary materials (rather than golden bronze or fine white marble), and it does not glorify the lowly hamburger. Although *Giant Hamburger* is certainly not beautiful or heroic, it is too large to be ignored. If you saw it outside a roadside diner, you might chuckle and stop in for lunch. But Oldenburg is a serious artist and this sculpture is owned by an art museum, so you can pretty safely assume that it must be about something besides hamburgers.

Can you imagine seeing the sculpture in a museum gallery alongside heroic figures of metal, stone, and wood? Is Oldenburg suggesting that artists should not take themselves too seriously? Perhaps he means that art should inspire humor, surprise, and innocent wonder—and that art should be about the things that really matter in a culture. Is Oldenburg saying that in America hamburgers are really important? Isn't the hamburger—cheap, convenient, and mass-produced—one of the great symbols of American life? By making it soft, almost shapeless, and from everyday materials, doesn't Oldenburg imply that it is an ordinary part of people's lives?

In art there is no right or wrong when it comes to subject matter, materials, or scale. An artist who can surprise you and make you think or feel something new is doing a good job, even if the object produced is odd or unattractive.

The Saint Padmasambhava,
artist unknown, Tibet, seventeenth century
Ivory, 5 1/2" x 3 1/2" x 2"

SMALL
SCALE

Sculptures that are huge, such as the Statue of Liberty, or that are unexpectedly large-scale, such as Oldenburg's *Giant Hamburger*, impress you by dominating their space.

A small-scale sculpture is more intimate and sometimes more involving because you have to study it carefully just to see what it is. A sculpture that pulls you in close draws you into its world of miniature detail.

This small ivory statue represents a historical figure, Padmasambhava, a Buddhist saint who in the eighth century was invited by the king of Tibet to travel from his home in present-day Pakistan to Tibet to rid the country of dangerous demons.

If you look carefully, you can see that he is holding a full cup in his left hand and a double-pointed ritual implement, called a *dorje* (the Tibetan word for "thunderbolt") in his right hand. Padmasambhava is using the power of the thunderbolt to help destroy the demons. His eyebrows are drawn together in a scowl that shows his fierce concentration. Padmasambhava successfully removed the spirits through his special prayers and ritual acts. On his journey home he stopped in the neighboring Himalayan country of Bhutan and introduced the Buddhist religion.

Many other statues of Tibetan saints resemble this one, showing robed figures with legs crossed in a position of meditation. You can recognize that this one is Padmasambhava not only by his serious look and the objects he holds but also by his earrings, his unusual hat, and his cape.

The sculpture compels you to look at the details closely to determine who the figure is and what he is doing. Does that make you want to hold it in your hand? Can you imagine how it feels?

SCALE
AND MINIATURE WORLDS

Some small sculptures capture your attention by joining simple, everyday objects in unexpected groupings that seem mysterious and puzzling.

Joseph Cornell was an American artist known for sculptures that are called constructions or assemblages. He lived all his life in a small house in Flushing, Queens, in New York City, but he liked to take long walks alone through Manhattan, where he would find or buy the kinds of useless things that other people

Soap Bubble Set, Joseph Cornell, 1936
Glass containing map of the moon, goblet, egg, pipe, head, and four boxes, 15 3/4 " x 14 1/4" x 5 3/8"

overlooked: old pipes, stuffed birds, doll heads, watch faces, postcards, theater playbills, or used magazines. Cornell found great pleasure in arranging these discarded remnants inside small boxes, which resemble tiny stage sets or doll houses. The ways these simple objects are arranged suggest strange ideas and draw you into their miniature worlds.

If you look carefully, you can see that this box contains seven compartments divided by glass. At the top are four white wooden cylinders, two of them with pictures of the planet Saturn and medieval scenes. In the center is a French map of the Moon and a white clay pipe. At the bottom are three glass disks or lenses. On the left is an egg, painted blue and gold, in a glass. On the right is a doll, with its head painted blue and gold, on a white pedestal.

Cornell was fascinated with the mysteries of the universe. The otherworldly parts of this box seem to relate through some mysterious, heavenly magic. The Moon and Saturn are cosmic bodies that medieval people believed had an influence on human bodies. The egg, the Moon, and the doll head are similar shapes. What connection could there be between them? Why are the head and the egg both painted blue with touches of gold?

What do the glass disks at the bottom of this box suggest to you? Could they be telescope lenses or the dishes for scientific experiments? When you look at other works by Cornell, you get some idea of his favorite themes. One was soap bubbles, which can look like tiny transparent planets floating in the air. Here, the pipe seems to be blowing a bubble in the shape of the Moon.

There may have been specific stories in Cornell's mind when he made these boxes, but the most important thing is the way they create a wondrous mood. The box is like a puzzle, or a game for which you have lost the rules. It fits together, but it is hard to say exactly why.

The Roden Crater Project, James Turrell, ongoing

GIANT SCALE

Cornell's sculpture, small enough to hold, is a mystery world in a box. Some sculptures at the other end of the size scale are so enormous that you cannot see them completely except from the air.

In the desert of Arizona an American artist, James Turrell, is working on a project that, from one point of view, could be called the world's largest sculpture. In 1974 he spent six months flying his own airplane over an area filled with the conical remains of volcanoes that erupted around 500,000 years ago. He chose one, called Roden Crater, to be a viewing platform for the sky and the stars.

Roden Crater sits high on the edge of a plateau overlooking the distant ridges of the Painted Desert. The land around the crater is used for grazing cattle, and wild elk sometimes wander by this isolated spot. Turrell is smoothing and rounding the crater's upper rim to appear like a bowl. He is removing distractions so that people who enter the bowl will see only its gentle sloping walls of sand topped by the great blue bowl of the sky.

When nothing is left but earth and sky, Roden Crater becomes a kind of lens that focuses our attention on the celestial events happening around us all the time. You know that the sun rises and sets every day, but how often do you actually see this cosmic occurrence from beginning to end or notice the purple shadow that rises off the earth at sunset and sweeps across the skies? At night the stars appear to close in and hover just above the volcano's rim. Roden Crater gently shapes the perceptions of anyone who steps into its deliberately simplified form for a few hours. How big, would you say, is a sculpture that incorporates the earth below it and includes the stars and space above it?

Eventually, Turrell will add tunnels, chambers, and viewing spaces that will turn the crater into an artistic observatory, somewhat like the ancient monument of Stonehenge in England. Some of these spaces will be filled with a rich, textured light that will seem like something you could touch. All of them will use the special qualities of the location to increase your perception of light and space.

Turrell was able to get a good head start on this massive artwork by choosing a crater that volcanic forces had already roughly shaped, in the same way that Isamu Noguchi began his sculpture *Unidentified Object* by choosing a very interesting rock. But Turrell's changes and additions are so ambitious that this unusual work will not be finished for many years, probably not until sometime in the next century. When it is, it will be one of the world's most amazing sculptures.

SURFACE

A problem with seeing sculpture in a museum is that you are almost never allowed to touch it. The rules are understandable: The museum must protect and preserve art for the future. If thousands of people touch a work of art, the oils from their hands will discolor or destroy the sculpture's surface, and eventually it will wear down or break. Still, keeping your distance feels unnatural. Many sculptures beg to be touched, depending on the materials from which they are made.

The appearance of the sculpture's surface can be as important as the way it feels. Is it regular or irregular? Smooth or rough? Shiny or dull? A regular, smooth, shiny surface can make a sculpture look pure, precious, and eternal, whereas an irregular, rough, dull surface can make a sculpture seem crude and temporary.

TOUCH

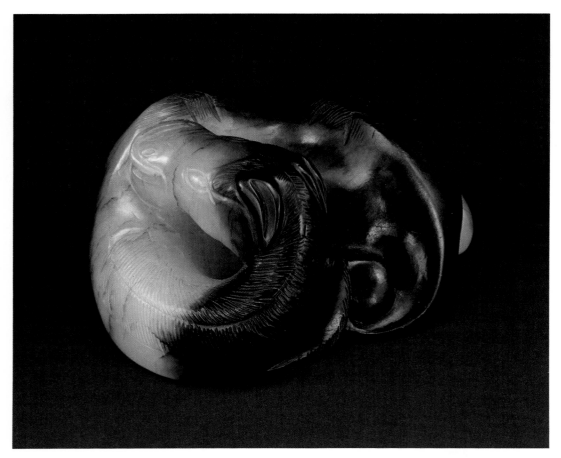

Reclining Camel, unknown artist, China, third to tenth century
Jade, 1 1/8" x 2 3/8" x 2"

Jade carvings are usually very smooth and pleasant to touch. Jade is a translucent stone that is so hard that it cannot be cut with metal but must be worn away by grinding. Chinese artists were making elegant jade carvings as long ago as six thousand years.

The ancient Chinese believed that jade had magical power, and they would often place jade carvings in graves to try to keep the bodies of the dead from decaying. They also thought that jade symbolized the virtues of an ideal person: Its smooth surface represented kindness, its hardness represented intelligence, and its translucency represented honesty.

This carving shows a camel sitting down and stretching its neck over its back. The sculpture is small enough to be easily held in your hand. Notice how the camel's ears have been flattened back so that they will not protrude. Some texture has been added by incising, or cutting, lines of hair in the camel's neck and down its back. Do you want to hold this camel in your hand? If you were able to touch it, you could run your thumb along its gentle curves.

A carving such as this one had no practical purpose and was not meant to tell a particular story. The first owner of this jade probably thought of camels as slightly exotic, like most of us do today, and he or she probably enjoyed the amusing, lively look of the animal. The sculpture was an object of luxury and pleasure meant to be treasured and enjoyed privately.

Is this a sculpture that you would like to touch? It is studded all over with nails, blades, and sharp metal pieces that have been driven into it.

A sculpture of an oath-taking figure made by an artist of the Kongo culture in Africa was considered too dangerous to belong to a single individual, so the statue belonged to a whole village and was kept in a special place under the care of a priest. When the village needed protection, or when someone wanted to swear an oath or prove guilt or innocence, nails were driven into the wooden figure to enrage and activate it. The figure must have been thought to be very powerful and effective, because it accumulated so much metal.

The carver only started the process of making this object when he shaped the wooden body. The bristling surface that you now see is the collaborative result of many people adding to it over an extended period of time. The nails were inserted not for artistic reasons but for

ANIMATED SURFACE

the practical reason of arousing the power of the figure. However, they have a very strong artistic effect. You do not have to be a believer in the religion that motivated this work to realize that this figure represents a fierce, mysterious force. His raised arm probably held a weapon of some kind. The box in his belly held medicines.

Because of the unusual surface, energy seems to fly out of this figure like sparks from a grinding wheel. Time has also played an important role in shaping its appearance. The metal parts rusted into a reddish brown color that nearly matches the wood, and the paint on the face was worn and faded probably long before the figure was acquired by a museum in 1892. The surfaces of sculptures often change over centuries unless they are carefully preserved and protected. Some sculptors intend for this to happen. Others would probably be very surprised to see how their work looks today.

Oath-Taking Figure, unknown artist, Congo, nineteenth century
Wood, nails, cloth, tacks, glass, and paint, height: 26"

THE PERFECT SURFACE

One of the first things that you notice about this sculpture is its gleaming color. The marble is so white that it almost seems to glow from inside. The bright, polished surface conveys a feeling of calm and eternal perfection.

The sculpture portrays an imagined moment after the crucifixion of Jesus when his dead body was given to his mother, Mary. She holds him in her lap with her right hand and looks down thoughtfully. Her left hand reaches out in a graceful gesture that is hard to understand at first. What do you think it indicates? Sorrow? Acceptance? Distress? Confusion? Try making the same shape with your left hand and see how it feels.

When you see this sculpture, you can hardly believe it is carved out of stone. Look at the way the fingers of Mary's right hand press into the cloth and raise the flesh of Christ's shoulder. The fabric of Mary's robe is bunched,

Pietà, Michelangelo, 1498–99
Marble, height: 68 1/2"

44

wrinkled, and folded. There are veins on Jesus' body and subtle suggestions of his ribs. Every muscle and hair is completely convincing.

It seems as if Michelangelo wanted to make us feel that we were actually there at that moment when Jesus was taken down from the cross. But does this sculpture look truly lifelike to you? What's missing?

Around the same time that Michelangelo made the Pietà in Italy, artists in Germany were making sculptures of the same subject out of wood that they painted. Would you feel different about Michelangelo's Pietà if it were painted and you could not see that it was made of marble? It might look more lifelike that way, but would it be as great a work of art?

Michelangelo wanted his sculpture to appear lifelike and abstract at the same time. The gleaming, eternally white surface of the marble helps make the religious point that the death of Jesus had a universal significance beyond time.

This, one of the most famous sculptures in the world, was carved by Michelangelo when he was only twenty-five years old. When the Pietà was finished, around 1500, Michelangelo's contemporaries were amazed by how beautiful it was, although some criticized him for making Mary so young. What do you think of this sculpture?

Man Pointing, Alberto Giacometti, 1947
Bronze, 70 1/2" x 40 3/4" x 16 3/8"

IRREGULAR SURFACE

Just by looking, we can often recognize soft and hard, rough and smooth, and sometimes even hot and cold. We can tell the difference between materials and can frequently judge whether something is new or old. A sculptor can manipulate our perceptions, as in this figure of a man pointing, which was made by Alberto Giacometti.

This bronze sculpture is life-size but incredibly thin. Even a skeleton would be thicker. And the man seems elongated, or stretched out, especially in his legs and arms. The skin of the figure is so irregular that it is hard to tell the difference between the rough bumps along the surface and his features. In fact, the bumpiness of the surface makes it difficult to see the man clearly. It is as if you were looking at someone through wavy glass. The general shape is clear enough, but the details are obscure.

The figure was cast in bronze from a model that Giacometti made by attaching pieces of clay or plaster to sticks. If someone asked you why the surface is so rough, you could say that these are the marks left by the hands of the sculptor as he put it together. But the irregularity also looks like the result of erosion and decay over a long time so that the figure resembles an ancient deity, or god, discovered by an archaeological dig.

The rough surface helps this sculpture remain mysterious and vague. When you look for clues that would help you identify him, the irregular surface keeps you from finding them. Is the man naked or dressed? Old or young? Why is he pointing? Is he happy? Angry? Commanding? Does he look to you as if he has been squeezed thin by the space around him? Or do you feel that his outstretched arms are taking charge of the space around him? He is an isolated, nearly featureless figure who seems to be pointing to something important, but how can you tell what it is?

Becca, David Smith, 1965
Stainless steel, 113 1/4" x 123" x 30 1/2"

FINISH

David Smith's sculpture *Becca* is made of stainless steel plates that were welded together. After the work was assembled the artist took a power grinder and moved it all over the surface, leaving spiraling tracks of very tiny grooves that catch and reflect the light. These circular polish marks give the sculpture a dynamic glow.

The swirls left on the steel by the grinder are impossible to photograph because you have to be moving to appreciate them. As you shift position, the light reflects off them from different angles, making some lines disappear and others flash brilliantly like neon. This effect is especially strong outdoors in bright sunlight.

The sculpture is built out of flat planes that seem lightweight, as though they could fly in the air. There are back and front views but no side view to speak of. *Becca*'s composition is very simple: two horizontal plates, one slightly longer than the other; four diagonal plates; and a vertical post holding the work to its base. The sculpture has dignity and presence that come from its size (nearly ten feet tall) and the way it is balanced. Notice that the "feet" extend beyond the base, like Rodin's *Monument to Balzac*. Yet the silvery polish gives the heavy planes the glinting colors of the sky and makes them seem bright and free.

Because the shape is so regular, it looks almost like an abstract symbol somewhere between an H and an X. Could the diagonal plates be arms and legs? Does this look to you anything like a person dancing? If archaeologists dug this up thousands of year from now, they might imagine that it had some secret religious meaning. But Smith named *Becca* after his eleven-year-old daughter. Now that you know this, do you think this sculpture might be a portrait?

Smith wanted to express his feelings about his daughter in an abstract language that would describe her qualities (brightness, freedom, joy) without limiting himself to a literal picture of her features.

CONTEXT

Because a sculpture occupies and influences the space around it, its effect and meaning can change when its surroundings change. A sculpture is just one element within a larger environment, and it interacts with what is around it—including you, the viewer.

For thousands of years in the Western tradition, all sculptures were images of people, animals, or gods and were elevated on pedestals or on the walls of buildings. In the twentieth century, however, the definition of sculpture expanded.

Today, a sculpture can also be an everyday object selected by the artist and placed on a pedestal, a part of nature that is slightly altered, or even a whole environment created by the artist.

It is more important to use sculpture than to define it. A successful sculpture helps us change the way we think about or experience our world. Sculptures even have the special power to help us understand who we are and how we live.

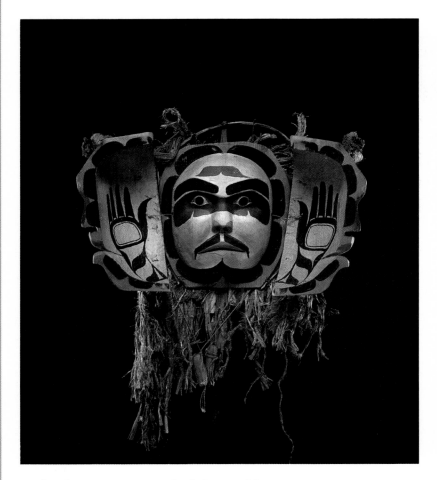

Mask of Born-to-Be-Head-of-the-World, unknown Kwakiutl artist,
Canada, nineteenth century
Wood, red and undyed cedar bark, and rope, 29 1/2" x 24 3/8" x 9"

The two photographs are of the same mask. The right-hand photograph depicts its closed position, and the left-hand photograph reveals another face inside, visible when the mask is open. This mask was made around one hundred years ago by a Native American artist, a member of the Kwakiutl, who live on Vancouver Island in British Columbia, Canada.

It took a very skilled artist to make this beautiful, clever mask showing a man with a mustache and beard who wears an eye mask. What are the differences between the outer face and the inner face? Which one is more expressive and animated? Which one is more intense and mysterious?

Your experience of this mask would be very different if you saw it in use. It was carved to be worn by a dancer describing the story of a man named Siwidi. When Siwidi was a young man he was dragged by an octopus into the lake where the chief of the undersea kingdom lived. This chief sent Siwidi on adventures visiting the tribes that live in the sea. Finally, he returned to his people as a hero with supernatural powers and was renamed Born-to-Be-Head-of-the-World.

The closed and open versions show two forms of the hero. The lips on the closed mask are shaped as if he were talking or singing. Imagine how dramatic it must have been when the dancer who wore this mask, with its hair moving from side to side, suddenly flung the mask open to reveal the bright inner image of the transformed hero.

The mask by itself is incomplete. It needs the dancer and the music to look the way it was meant to look, but it should also have the proper setting, including the woods of the Pacific Northwest and an appreciative audience that understands the details of Siwidi's story.

SETTING AND USE

Poseidon of Artemisium, unknown
artist, Greece, ca. 460 B.C.
Bronze, height: 83"

Sometimes the original function of a sculpture has been lost or forgotten, so you cannot fully understand what it meant to the artist who made it or to the people who first saw it. There is no one left to tell the story.

A six-and-a-half-foot-tall bronze sculpture was found in 1928 in the sea near a Greek island. The figure is so heroic and beautiful that it probably represents a god. The date of its creation was estimated by comparing it to other bronzes. No one knows how it came to be in the sea. Maybe it was being delivered to a temple soon after it was made. Or maybe it was being exported as an art treasure many centuries later.

Originally, the statue must have held a weapon of some kind in its right hand. If it was a trident, a three-pronged spear, then the statue is Poseidon, god of the sea, who helped save the Greeks from an attack by a Persian fleet a few years before the statue was made. If it was a thunderbolt, then the statue is Zeus, the most important Greek god, the source of divine power.

The original function of this sculpture has been lost. No one knows where it stood or how it was used. What must have seemed obvious to those who made it—such as whom the weapon is aimed at—is now just a matter of speculation. You do not know the story that this sculpture represents. Imagine how much you would be missing if you saw Michelangelo's Pietà but did not know the story of Jesus.

You can still admire the skill of the artist who made this bronze. Notice the fingers of the left hand, which seem to project an invisible force out of the straight left arm. And don't miss the slight lift of his left toes, which expresses the tension just before the moment of release. You would not want to be this god's target!

Try comparing this sculpture to Giacometti's *Man Pointing*. The Greek god, with a surface that shows every muscle and vein in clear detail, is an individual, if idealized. His pose indicates power and decisiveness. Giacometti's modern man is anonymous and abstract. His pointing suggests hesitation and indecision. Do you think that these differences reflect cultural changes over the 2,500 years between these two sculptures, or are they just coincidences?

THE MISSING STORY

RESPONSE

Some sculptures derive their power from their ability to change the way you feel about the environment around them.

Tilted Arc is amazingly simple yet very powerful. It consists of a 12-foot-high, 120-foot-long wall of rusted steel that is slightly curved and slightly tilted. The sculpture was commissioned to be installed in Federal Plaza, a vast plaza in downtown New York City. The building that fronts on the plaza contains federal government offices.

When *Tilted Arc* was installed, it dominated the plaza. Unlike many large sculptures in public places, this one was impossible to ignore when crossing the plaza from the street to the buildings. Walking around it required a deliberate effort. This made the sculpture unpopular with some of the office workers.

When installed in the plaza the work forced the viewers to be aware of their environment. As an object, it was clearly out of place. Because of its strong rust color, people noticed that all the buildings around it and the plaza itself were made of stone or shiny metal and that the major color in this part of the city is gray. Its curving shape made one realize that all the other objects in the area are built with straight lines and right angles. It even made one think about sound. The tilt and curve of the wall made it a reflector of sound. When people stood next to *Tilted Arc*, they heard the noise of the city changed to a steady rumbling, like the constant whooshing of a waterfall.

Imagine if you walked out of your house one morning and *Tilted Arc* was standing in the middle of the street on which you live. How would you feel about it? Would you think of it as some huge, rusty steel thing inconveniently blocking the street? Would you wonder why it was there? Would you use it as a backstop for ball games? Or would you suddenly notice the color of your neighborhood, the lines of its buildings, and its sounds?

Unfortunately, too few people enjoyed *Tilted Arc* at Federal Plaza, and it was removed.

Tilted Arc, Richard Serra, 1981–89
Cor-ten steel, 12' x 120' x 2 1/2"

INTERACTION

A new kind of sculpture, called installation art, has become increasingly common in the last thirty years. Installations are essentially room-size sculptures in which the work forms its own environment. Instead of reacting to an object from the outside, you actually become part of the sculpture as you walk through it. These installations are usually built just for specific exhibitions and then taken apart.

The installation *What It's Like, What It Is, 3* was made for an exhibition called Dislocations held from October 1991 to January 1992 at the Museum of Modern Art in New York. The work, by Adrian Piper, was a small, completely white room with four tiers of seats around the walls, like bleachers. At the top level a strip of mirror circled the room. In the center of the room was a tall white column with four video screens, one on each side. The room was very strongly lit and looked blazingly clean and bright. The video showed a black man standing against a black background. He faced the camera, then turned to the side, then to the back and to the other side as he said, "I'm not pushy. I'm not sneaky. I'm not rowdy. I'm not horny. I'm not scary. I'm not shiftless. I'm not crazy. I'm not servile.

I'm not stupid. I'm not dirty. I'm not smelly. I'm not childish. I'm not evil."

The room was so white that those who went into it seemed out of place and exposed, like specimens in a laboratory. Consequently, many visitors to the museum just looked in from the doorway. If they entered, they became part of the sculpture. If they sat in the top tier of seats, where the video could best be seen, they were able to see themselves in the mirror that encircled the room.

The video was there to remind people that everyone tends to form mental stereotypes of others, especially about those who belong to a different race or nation. These stereotypes are unfair because each person is an individual and should be treated justly and equally.

How would you feel sitting in a room like this? Would it make you think about injustice? Adrian Piper is an artist who believes that a person's emotional and intellectual experiences with art can help make him or her a better person. Do you agree?

What It's Like, What It Is, 3, Adrian Piper, 1991
Mixed media installation, size variable

INDEX